Unleashing Your Greatness

Buhle Dlamini

ISBN 10: 1508483876
ISBN-13: 978-1508483878

Buhle Dlamini

CONTENTS

Buhle Dlamini

ACKNOWLEDGMENTS

On this journey to unleashing my own greatness I have been blessed with an incredible life partner, my beautiful wife Stacey that I was privileged to meet as a young 17-year-old and got to marry at 23. You have been a pillar of strength in times of great trials and a source of joy as we have celebrated life together. I know that I would not have come as far as I have without your support, encouragement and occasional rebuke when my ego and pride gets away with me. I am grateful for your pearls of wisdom, challenging questions and reassuring belief in my ability to make things happen.

I am grateful for the support of friends that have been stuck with me from my youth. Rob Wright, Olefile Masangane, Seth Naicker, Quinton Pretorius and recently Perez 'Cherry' Mpio. Thanks for keeping up with my restless spirit in pursuit of greatness and for always stepping in to help me be who I can be. My mentors, Bennie Harms and Garth Japhet, for seeing the 'special' in me and entrusting me with responsibilities to draw it out, thank you!

My family, all of you, thanks! But I want to single out those who have been my parents after losing my own. Mama Busi and Baba Mlungisi Qwabe, although you are my Aunt and Uncle you stepped in and parented me when my parents passed away. Knowing that I could always go to you and be 'home' has been a gift I cannot begin to describe. I love you and thank you. Fred and Shirley Jeffery, you became more than my parents-in-law but you have carried my family and me and been a pillar of love and strength. Thanks to Wayne and Charlene MacLean for being my adopted Canadian parents and for all the love you have showered my children with.

Lastly, my Gogo (my maternal grandmother) Grace Khumalo for helping me unleash my greatness as a young man and instilling strong faith in God and myself. I love you and dedicate all I have achieved to your incredible sacrifices so that I could be where I am today.

Preface

Unleashing Greatness One Person At A Time

Buhle Dlamini

As a professional speaker, when asked what it is that I do, my answer should always be "I am in the business of unleashing greatness." That is exactly what I do - Unleash Greatness in others. All of us are born with seeds of greatness inside of us regardless of who we are, or where we come from, and our greatest mission in life is to unleash the greatness within and change the world around us in the process. As humans, we have unlimited potential to achieve great things. Thomas Edison, who among other inventions, gave us the light bulb, the movie camera and the rechargeable battery once said:

"If we did all the things we are capable of, we would literally astound ourselves."

Have you astounded yourself lately? As a speaker, I am often invited to speak at numerous conferences and organizations around the world and my job is to help individuals, businesses and organizations tap into this great potential with every presentation I do. I challenge people to believe in their own abilities, change their perceptions about what's possible for them and guide them to their true greatness.

The world we live in has a way of beating the sense of wonder and possibility out of us. We grow up in the world that tells us that there is no point in chasing dreams and our experiences and failures along the way further entrench this belief. Until someone comes along and shakes us up, our potential remains buried. That is why I have written this book, to reach more people like you, whether you get to hear my message live as part of an audience or not. I want to challenge you to rise above your current reality, to see and believe what could be, and set you on track to make it happen for yourself.

I grew up in a rural, impoverished Zulu village in Apartheid South Africa, and lost both my parents at a young age. I personally know adversity. If you had told me growing up that I would become an entrepreneur, a global speaker and an author I would not have believed you. I had to unleash my own greatness and rise above my challenges and limitations so that I can be an inspiration to others. So, as I continually unleash my own greatness and push myself to be the best I can be, I pass the challenge to you. This book will help you with the how.

Buhle Dlamini

Introduction

Greatness

It's What's In You

"All of us are born with great potential, but not all of us turn that potential into performance."

Have you ever seen something great and asked yourself "how can something so amazing come from there?" The greatest humanitarian in modern history was found serving in the slums of Calcutta, India. There she was; among the sick and the dying in the most unattractive part of the world, and yet many from all over came to learn from her. Mother Theresa was canonized in 2016 as Saint Theresa of Calcutta. This Albanian nun that moved to the slums of India to serve the most vulnerable, choosing a simple life for herself, became the modern-day Saint for generations to emulate.

Greatness is not measured by how famous or how wealthy one is. As a matter of fact, some of the richest people in our world today are among the least that we would want to emulate. How is that possible, when we are living in the age of 24/7 news and money seems to make the world go round? I think that deep down we all know that there is something more powerful, more worthy of our pursuit than fame and fortune. Yes, some of the great people of our time are rich and famous and some hold high offices of power. But overall, greatness is not limited to the confines of the select few and that is why we all can achieve and unleash greatness in our own lives.

So, then what is greatness?

Greatness is a way of being and not merely a list of achievements. As Saint Theresa of Calcutta once said "Not all of us can achieve great things but all of us can do small things with great love"

Greatness is all around us. Stephen Covey writes in his book Everyday Greatness - "Greatness is a way of living, not a one-time event. It says more about who a person is than what a person has…"

"Not all of us can achieve great things but all of us can do small things with great love" - Saint Theresa of Calcutta

Every day, we encounter greatness in the service we receive from a small privately owned restaurant, or in a police officer who goes out of his way to be helpful, and in a teacher that gives more than is required. You know greatness when you encounter it, because it impacts you in some way. Greatness leaves an impact.

I grew up in rural village in Zulu land, South Africa. I was raised by my grandmother and she saw greatness in a young boy. She helped me to understand, from a very young age, that it doesn't matter where you come from, it doesn't matter what circumstances surround you, it's what's in you that counts!

It's What's In You That Counts!

We are all born with something to share with the world. All of us have within us the ability to shape the world around us in big and small ways. We all come into to this world entrusted with a unique offering to share with those around us, but not all us tap into the greatness inside of us.

The great Scottish Poet, John Buchan put it this way, "Our task is not to put greatness back into humanity, but to elicit it, for greatness is there already." The biggest challenge for all of us is to go about the work of eliciting the greatness that lies within us. Every day is an opportunity to bring out the greatness that lies untapped.

Here is a fact:

Not all of us are going to be rich, famous or run a country, but all of us can be great at what we do!

This is exactly why you picked up this book, because deep down you yearn to be all you can be. You desire to live your life to the full and make an impact with your life, business or career. Henry David Thoreau famously stated in Walden *"the mass of men lead lives of quiet desperation."* This is what happens when we fail to tap into what's truly possible for us, we lead lives of quiet desperation. Lives that are resigned to fate and circumstance; instead of creating what is possible for us.

I too could have chosen this route. I could have accepted that being born black in Apartheid South Africa and growing up in an impoverished village meant my life would be confined by those circumstances. I could have taken losing both my parents at a young age as a reason for me to choose a life of pity. But I refused to allow my circumstances to determine my future. I chose to unleash my greatness. I chose to live a life larger than my background dictated. I chose to rise to the levels that are possible for me, and that made all the difference.

You too can decide your own fate. Do you choose to unleash your greatness and accept the responsibility that is yours in making this a reality? If so, I invite you to come along as we unpack the five keys to **Unleashing Your Greatness** in the following chapters.

Buhle Dlamini

Section 1: Be Who You Be

The first key to unleashing your greatness is: Be Who You Be!

During my presentations, I get my audience to say this phrase after me **"Be Who You Be!"** I love the puzzled looks that I get, as I am sure you have one on your face right now. What am I going on about? Be Who You Be?

One of the things I enjoy about my travels around the world is that I get to meet and interact with different people. One of the places I love traveling to is the USA. When in the US, I enjoy hanging out with African Americans. I love the way they speak, especially among themselves. They put a twist on things. Instead of saying 'Be who you want to be' they say 'Be Who You Be Maaan!'

There is just something so catchy, and so cool about how that sounds, but for me there is a deeper meaning to this phrase. **Be Who You Be,** speaks to the fact that to unleash your greatness you need to:

Embrace Who You *Are* and Embrace Who You *Can* Be

To truly tap into *Your* Greatness the answer lies in how you embrace who you are right now, but going further to also embrace who you can be. It's about embracing the *current* you and the *possible* you! The *current* you is shaped by your background, your history, and your experiences which have brought you to this point in time. The *possible* you will be shaped by the choices you make, the talents you develop and the purpose you pursue. Are you ready to tap into who you are and who you can become?

IDENTITY

1. Embrace Who You Are

"To be yourself in a world that is constantly trying to make you something else is the greatest accomplishment."

-Ralph Waldo Emerson

We live in a world of comparisons. From the time, you are born you are constantly compared to someone in one way or another. And as result we start measuring ourselves based on how we measure up to someone else. We spend too much time comparing ourselves to others. We look at what other people earn, what cars they drive, what houses they live in and what clothes they wear. Even our decisions about what we want to achieve with our own lives are usually heavily influenced by the comparison game.

Well, it's time for you to put on the breaks, stop and evaluate your own life. Where has all this comparison brought you to? Do you believe that the best for you is keeping up with the Joneses next door? I know you are getting the idea here. You cannot unleash your greatness by trying to be like someone else.

Embracing who you are is the foundation of Unleashing Your Greatness. I learned this lesson when I was in high school back in Hlabisa where I grew up. I had won an award for a science project I did in my region and an official from the Education Department was coming to my school to present me with the certificate. It was going to be a big affair and a special school assembly was to be held for me and others to receive our accolades in front of the whole school.

Instead of being filled with excitement, I was totally mortified. You see, my shoes were torn and they were the only pair I owned. I was not unique in this regard, many other kids at our school had a similar challenge due to the financial situation of many families in the village. However, the moment you were singled out for special attention, it was common for others to make fun of you. So, I did not look forward to being on that stage.

Something in my countenance must have betrayed me, because when I got home that afternoon my Grandmother asked me what was wrong? I told her the great news about my award and the presentation that was to follow the next day. She was surprised as to why I was not as thrilled as I should have been. I told her about how I did not want to be on that stage because of my torn shoes. I was ashamed and embarrassed. Without showing too much emotion, she jumped into action and went to speak to my Grandfather about me using his shoes for the big occasion.

My Grandfather pulled out his 'special shoes', the ones he wore for special occasions. There were two-toned, black and white and he handed them over to me to try. I tried them on, but there was a problem. They were too big for me. Without missing a beat my grandmother jumped into action and got some old newspapers and started stuffing them in the front part of the shoes and got me to try them on. I did and they fit me well.

She asked me how they felt and I started tearing up as I said 'they fit well Gogo'. I didn't know why I cried then. I think it was because I was feeling sorry for myself, that I didn't have nice shoes like some of the other kids at school who got new shoes every year. I felt sorry for myself because I had to put on my old man's shoes to go to a special event. I felt sorry for myself because it just didn't seem fair, why me?

I am sure you feel sorry for yourself from time to time. I am sure you feel that you should be much further in your career than you've gotten. You should have achieved more by now; you should have earned more. I am sure you know that feeling that life is just not fair. If you do, you can relate to what I was going through at that moment even though I did not have the words to describe it at the time.

My Grandmother's voice shook me from my pity-party when she said "Stop feeling sorry for yourself and remember that it is you who's going to be on that stage tomorrow and not all of those children you are comparing yourself to. You won that award. You did that and you will do more amazing things but never compare yourself to others."

Wow! If she could have it she would have said "Be Who You Be Maaan!"

At that moment, a revelation hit me. I cannot live my life by comparing myself to others, I must embrace who I am, give what I have and excel at being me!

You cannot unleash your greatness without first embracing who you are. Not who your parents wanted you to be. Not who your society groomed you to be. Not who your education trained you to be, but who you really are.

Embracing who you are is what sets you apart from everybody else. Your greatness begins when you realize that you are exactly what you need to be for what you are meant to achieve with your life. You are enough. Your experiences, even the painful ones, have brought you to where you are today. Your background has shaped you to know what you know so that you can do what only you can do. Greatness begins the moment you embrace the person that you are. Not looking at your short-comings, not focusing on your weak points but embracing the great things in you that only you can share with the world.

When this realization came to me it changed my future completely. I no longer felt sorry for myself or wasted another minute comparing myself to others and their gifts. Instead, I started focusing on my own strengths and gifts and everything changed. It is about time you do the same. Start embracing yourself as you are, recognizing that you have exactly what you need to unleash your greatness. Take some time now and look at the experiences that have shaped you, the talents that you have and embrace them as key elements to your success. Be Who You Be Maaan!

DISTINCTION

2. What Makes You Stand Out

"If a man is called to be a street sweeper, he should sweep streets even as a Michelangelo painted, or Beethoven composed music or Shakespeare wrote poetry. He should sweep streets so well that all the hosts of heaven and earth will pause to say, 'Here lived a great street sweeper who did his job well.'"

- Martin Luther King Jr.

The famous quote from Martin Luther King Jr says it all. It's not what you do that makes you great, it's doing what you do in a way that makes the world stop and notice that does. We can all find our distinction. Be Who You Be is all about distinguishing yourself for yourself.

What does that mean? *Distinguishing Yourself for Yourself?*

It's about making a choice that sets you apart for you to be the best you can be. You do this primarily for yourself and then for the world around you. When you take the time to carve out for yourself, your own playing field you become the master of your fate. Don't get me wrong here, I don't mean to imply that you are in control of what happens to you, but rather that you choose the direction in which you travel.

Great people understand early on that their greatness is determined by how they stand out from the crowd. By choosing to travel their own path and bucking the trend; they start down the road to their own greatness.

> **"I am the Greatest, I said that even before I knew I was." -Muhammad Ali**

Muhammad Ali (born Cassius Marcellus Clay Jr) has been widely regarded as one of the most significant and celebrated sports figures of the 20th century. Ali as a boxer was quick on his feet and completely outworked all his opponents. But this was not the only thing that made him stand out. There were many other African American boxers in the 60's but none were as 'Sassy' and sharp witted as Ali. He used his mouth and his quick feet and stamina to become the greatest of all time.

One of his famous quotes is "I am the greatest, I said that even before I knew I was." This tells us a great deal about Ali and his rise to unleashing his greatness. First, he was incredibly confident of his abilities. Secondly, that his confidence in his ability preceded the actual proof of them. Ali chose to be great. He chose to be great before he won one title, while he was practicing, he was already sure of his potential to be great. He talked and worked his way to success.

For young men like Muhammad Ali at the time, boxing was a way out, but he recognized that it would be a platform to achieve even greater things. He used what set him apart to rise above the rest. Ali spoke truth to power when few black men of his era could. He used his talent in boxing as a launching pad to challenge on all sorts of issues. He opposed the Vietnam war and publicly refused to be conscripted by the US Military. For this he paid a heavy price as he was eventually arrested, found guilty of draft evasion charges and stripped of his boxing titles. He appealed to the Supreme Court and succeeded but had already lost four of his best boxing years.

Ali wasn't the greatest sports figure of the 20th century because of his boxing talent alone, he became the greatest because of his ability to speak up and challenge where few others did. He earned the respect of people the world over because he used what he had and used it to the best of his ability.

We become great when we tap into our distinction, when we uncover that which makes us stand out from the crowd.

> **"Don't become a wandering generality. Be a meaningful specific." - Zig Ziglar**

You tap into your greatness the moment you learn to distinguish yourself. Many people are happy to just be an accountant, to be a realtor and to be a doctor. But the greatest among us do not let their professions define who they are. They; instead, choose to distinguish themselves by tapping into their uniqueness. Consider the following example:

The amazing doctor who prides himself in personally connecting with every single patient that he treats, even though he sees dozens of patients a day. This doctor goes out of his way to remember specific personal details about his patients even though it is not required in the public hospital where he works. He makes it his personal mission not to treat them as patients but as friends, by choosing to connect beyond seeing them as just subjects. This doctor is gifted in his field but believes that his real distinction is connection. This makes him great!

This is just one example that no matter what profession you find yourself in you can '*Be Who You Be'* by finding a way to stand out and be great. I have met waiters that make me want to go back to the same restaurant, not just because the food is great but because the experience by them is great. I am sure you know of many other people in many different professions that stand out because they choose to Be Who They Be and stand out from the crowd.

When you discover what it is that sets you apart, and what makes you stand out from the crowd, you find your distinction. As a speaker, I quickly realized that for me, what made me stand out was my ability to connect with people on a personal basis. I have spoken to audiences of 10 people and more than 3000 and yet the response I always get is "I could relate to this guy; he spoke to me personally." I have been tempted many times to change my style to be more like other speakers who impress with their smarts and style but it's just not me. I am the greatest when I use my distinction and stand out from the crowd. The same applies for you. What is it that distinguishes you from so many others who do what you do?

MASTERY

3. Optimize What You Have

"Use what talents you possess; the woods would be very silent if no birds sang there except those that sang best."

- Henry Van Dyke

All humans throughout history that have left their footprint in the sands of time have been individuals who understood the importance of mastering their own gifts and talents. Everyone, yes, everyone has a talent. Don't buy the lie that many tell themselves, 'I don't have any talents to speak of'. This is a myth that is perpetuated by our culture of hero-worshipping few individuals because they get the right press and attention. We are all endowed with amazing gifts, the sad truth is that very few of us take the time to develop what we have.

Tell me, what comes to mind when you think of talent? Most people immediately start thinking about the arts; music, painting, dancing, etc. Sure, there is a lot of talent associated with the arts. The next category that comes to mind when one thinks of talent is sports; like tennis, football, hockey, athletics, etc. But few rarely look beyond these two fields to find their unique talents. Talent manifests itself in many forms. A talent or gift is any ability that an individual finds relatively easy and enjoyable to do compared to other activities.

We grow up in environments that puts too much focus on certain types of talents and little or none on other talents. Thus, many people live their whole lives without truly revealing who they are and what they can share with the world. To unleash your true greatness, you need to take some time identifying and then developing your unique talent or gift. Granted your own talent might not get you on the front pages of magazines or on television but maximizing your gift is one of the ways to live your best life.

Maximizing your talent or gift is about living up to your strengths. Lately there has been a lot of focus on maximizing your strengths to live your best life. When we were growing up we were taught to spend more time working on bettering our weak points. Your teacher most likely wrote letters to your parents on how you needed to spend more time working on your math if it was your weakest subject. Rarely, did we ever hear the words 'you are doing so well in debate class, you should spend as much time developing your communication skills to be the best!' This is the problem with our society. We groom young people in our schools to be 'rounded' individuals so that few truly excel at anything.

Decide to become a master at something that you do better than most. Decide to work more on something that you enjoy and that brings you joy. Decide to spend more time arranging flowers because that is what you find so much joy doing. Decide to spend more time balancing budgets because that is what truly makes you come alive. Decide to optimize that which comes easy to you but difficult for others.

This is often hard to do because we have certain expectations placed upon us. Whether it is by our employers, our family responsibilities, our society or mostly by ourselves, it is hard to decide to go against the grain. I know this because somewhere along my journey I had to stop trying to please everybody and started chasing and pursuing my gift and talent.

Decide to optimize that which comes easy to you but difficult for others.

Upon finishing high school, I started my studies in Analytical Chemistry. I had good grades in Math and Science and upon researching the fields available, one that made sense and paid good money was Analytical Chemistry. With that degree, I could work in quality assurance in almost any laboratory for most companies that manufacture anything from the food industry to chemicals and more. There was a lot of expectation from my family to pursue a field that would bring honor and guarantee good income for the future.

But, there was a problem. The more time I spent in the laboratory, the more I hated it. I just couldn't stand solving similar problems and testing chemicals for PH levels and working out compositions of elements. Though it was at times mentally stimulating and definitely challenging, I just did not enjoy it.

What I was passionate about was connecting with people. I loved helping people understand concepts and I had a desire to help people reach their potential. I particularly loved the idea of helping young people see possibility and inspire them to be the best they could be. I loved sharing inspirational stories that motivated people or just encouraged them. I loved making people laugh, learn and grow. Back then I didn't have this figured out as clearly as I have just described and so during my second year of college I found myself struggling. I struggled to find motivation for what I was doing. I dragged my feet and dreaded every day of study and work.

Finally, I spoke to counsellors and some of them helped me to explore what I wanted to do. So, at the end of my second year I took a very bold step, that was not very popular with my family. I decided to take a gap-year volunteering as a youth development worker with The Salvation Army. And, I came alive! I was trained in using drama, music and spoken word to inspire youth in schools, community centers and churches around the country. Something clicked inside me and I became a better communicator, motivator and trainer.

The rest, as they say is history. As I spent more time developing my skills; opportunities followed. The very next year, another opportunity to be in an international youth development team came and I worked with youth in Germany, UK and USA. Here I was, this boy from rural

Hlabisa in Zululand South Africa, who'd never even been on a plane, traveling to Germany and learning to inspire youth in another language! I never turned back, upon my return I decided to study Youth Development at the University of South Africa and completed my diploma, while working in the field. I started my first consulting firm (at the age of 23) focused on personal development and within two years I was consulting with some big companies on people and leadership development. My company (Young & Able Ltd) grew to employ more than a dozen consultants and it now focuses on organizational culture, leadership development as well as diversity and inclusion.

All this happened because I dared to pursue my talent and maximize my gift. I believe it's not enough just to work on your talent but that you should take the time to have mastery over it. Mastery, is where your true greatness lies. Don't be happy to just use your talent but seek to become the master at what you do.

After a lifetime of distinguished achievements as a cellist, the renowned Pablo Casals, at eighty-five, continued to rise early and spend most of the day practicing his cello. When asked during an interview why he continued to practice five hours a day, Casals replied, 'Because I think I'm getting better.' Pablo Casals reminds us that true greatness comes from spending time mastering your talent by continually optimizing what you have.

The questions that remain for you are:

Have you identified what it is that you have, so you can share it with the world?

What is it that makes you come alive?

Are you maximizing your gift and sharing it with the world? If not, what is stopping you? What will you do to change this?

Master your talent and Be Who You Be Maaan!

PURPOSE

4. Understand Your Why

"Purpose is the quality we choose to shape our lives around."

- Richard J. Leider

Why is it that some people enjoy their work, create positive change and impact the world around them, while others work hard but dread every day of their lives? Simon Sinek believes that the biggest secret that great people tap into, lies in understanding their *why* they do what they do. I fully agree, nothing is more powerful in creating a great life, a great career, and even a great movement than a clear purpose. When your purpose is clear, then, everything else falls into place.

When leaders want to inspire us to achieve great things, they call us to pursue a purpose that is greater than the sum of the things we must do to get there. They give us a clear and a compelling WHY. When Martin Luther King Jr stood at the Lincoln Memorial in Washington DC with hundreds of thousands of men and women who had come from all over the country, he gave them a compelling why. When he articulated the 'Dream' in his 'I Have a Dream' speech he was giving activists the reason why they needed to keep working for civil rights.

What Dr. King understood, was that for many who were listening to him that day and many who would later follow his call, the task at hand would often be too hard. Many would have to face prison, while some would endure beatings and indeed some would pay with their own lives. He knew the cost was high. He knew the work would be hard. He knew that some days would be completely unbearable. But, if any of his followers had a compelling WHY the work had to be done, many would be willing bear the 'whatever' was thrown at them.

Have you sometimes woken up feeling like 'I don't want to go to work today, I just want to snuggle in my warm bed' but still got up anyway? Why did you get up? Because the consequences of not getting up would cost you too much. You get up because you need your job to pay the bills, to keep your kids in school and feed your family. The cost attached to not going to work for no reason is too high for you. This 'why' is compelling but mostly for negative reasons.

To unleash your greatness, you need to create the why that compels you and pulls you forward. The why that fills you with energy and excitement instead of dread. The why that inspires you to be better, to reach higher and achieve greater things.

> **"Far better it is to dare mighty things, to win glorious triumphs, even though checkered by failure... than to rank with those poor spirits who neither enjoy nor suffer much, because they live in a gray twilight that knows neither victory nor defeat." - Theodore Roosevelt**

Unfortunately, few people choose to live on purpose. Few people choose to live like they have something important to achieve with their lives. Many are just happy to live mundane lives. But the great ones among us know that there is more to life than just avoiding failure.

Finding your purpose is choosing to live a driven life, a daring life, a life of meaning, instead of just living in that 'gray twilight that knows neither victory nor defeat' as Theodore Roosevelt put it.

If you are a leader running an organization, a department or your own business the same applies to you. The clearer you can articulate the why you do what you do for your followers, the more successful you become.

Great organizations become great because of the clarity of their why. Take Nike for example, which is one of the biggest sports apparel manufacturers in the world. They sell running shoes, jogging pants, soccer shoes, basketball gear and more. But, this is not the reason they exist. What they make is not their why. They make great sporting gear but here is their stated WHY they do it:

BRING INSPIRATION AND INNOVATION TO EVERY ATHLETE* IN THE WORLD. *IF YOU HAVE A BODY, YOU ARE AN ATHLETE.

Notice how they never mention any of what they do but emphasize the WHY they do it? Because your purpose is not meant to constrain you but to free you. If their purpose was making running shoes it would limit everything to the WHAT they do, but by elevating their purpose to the WHY they do it, everything changes. Because they exist to bring inspiration and innovation to every athlete in the world (which in their definition includes everybody with a body) they can do many things that will lead to inspiration and innovation.

I challenge you to take some time to consider your WHY statement. It doesn't have to be fancy and it doesn't have to be profound but it does have to inspire you. Consider the change you want your life and work to make and the difference you want to make. Remember my story in the previous chapter, how I wanted to do more than just earning a good salary? I tapped into my purpose and my why? I wanted to inspire others to activate their potential and that has been my compelling why ever since.

My Purpose Is To Inspire Others To Activate Their Potential!

This single statement has guided my decisions, the projects I pursue and the work that I do. It is liberating, challenging and yet simple for me to understand it and to hold myself to it. With this simple purpose, I have launched successful businesses, helped create not-for-profit organizations that are impacting thousands of lives and written books that are read across the globe.

What will your compelling why enable you to do?

What greatness can be unleashed by you pursuing a purpose bigger than yourself?

I challenge you to take the time to find out.

Put It into Action:

Be Who You Be Statement

Now that you have gone through the first key to unleashing your greatness, now put into practice what you have learned. Be Who You Be is about Embracing Who You Are and Embracing Who You Can Be. To do this you need to:

- Embrace Who You Are
- Know What Makes You Stand Out
- Optimize What You Have
- Understand Your Why

Take some time to figure this out for yourself.

Embrace Who You Are:

When describing yourself, what do you say:

I am ....
Examples (Leader, Teacher, Advocate, Activist etc.)

Know What Makes You Stand Out:

The way you distinguish yourself from others like you:

I am very........ ....
Examples (Conscientious, Caring, Expressive, Focused etc.)

Optimize What You Have:

Your Unique Gift, Talent or Skill:

I am a gifted in...
Examples (Speaking, Singing, Writing, Organizing etc.)

Understand Your Why:

Your compelling WHY you do what you do:

My purpose is...

Section 2: Live Your Values

The second key to unleashing your greatness is: Live Your Values!

"I've learned that people will forget what you said, people will forget what you did, but people will never forget how you made them feel."

- Maya Angelou

Your greatness is determined more by what is inside you than what you say or do, because your values have a way of shining through. The truly great among us understand that it's your values, more than your words, that form the foundation of true greatness.

Values seem to be in fashion these days. More and more leaders and organizations are now emphasizing the importance of values. But values are much more than the latest fad, they guide the lifestyle and choices of those who transcend the mediocre existence in pursuit of personal greatness. Many of us think we understand our values but often we cannot describe them with clarity and certainty. In this section, we will look at what values are, and how we clarify our own to unleash greatness in our lives.

PRINCIPLE

---

5. What's On Your T-shirt?

It's not hard to make decisions when you know what your values are.
- Roy E. Disney

If you've ever been to a Football, Hockey or Soccer game you know the excitement of the fans as they come in numbers to support their team. It's easy to get swept up in the enthusiasm and the camaraderie you feel with your fellow team supporters. There are loud slogans that you shout at the top of your voice. There are songs that you sing without caring who is listening even if you can't carry a tune in a bucket. In those moments, your identity is linked with your team, you celebrate if they win and you cry when they lose. It doesn't matter that you don't know the name of the person next to you, all that matters is what's on their t-shirt. Because as long as their t-shirt has your team's name and logo they're all right.

The team t-shirt/jersey tells you that you are on the same side, that you care about the same thing. Somehow that t-shirt logo communicates more than just what it says. That's what values are like. They might not be visible like the t-shirt but they shine through everything you do.

So, **What's on Your T-Shirt?**

I am strong believer in the value of values. Back in 2002 I met Dr. Garth Japhet, a well-known social-entrepreneur in South Africa who founded an organization called Soul City. This organization uses mass media like TV and Radio to communicate health and community development issues using drama and stories. By the time I met Garth, Soul City was already operating across many countries in Africa with incredible results. When I met him he was just starting a whole new organization - Heartlines, that would use the same strategy to communicate and challenge the nation about living out values, using movies and TV dramas. So, I became one of the founding members of his new venture. At Heartlines we are driven by the belief that if we encourage people to not only know their values but live these out, we can deal with some of the biggest challenges we face in our country.

Most people seem to agree that a value like honesty and integrity is a good one but when you ask them if they are honest, well, that's a different story. So, we created films and TV dramas that would encourage people to engage with values that are important to them for them to live them out.

The campaign received great support from different sectors of society. We secured a partnership with the national broadcaster SABC (South African Broadcasting Corporation) as well as receiving funding from one of the big banks. We also felt that it would be important to get a public endorsement from a national figure. So, in 2006 the former President, Nelson Mandela, agreed to be on the opening sequence of our films. This was quite a massive undertaking and we couldn't have been more thrilled about the news.

Meeting Mandela

As director for television drama it fell upon me to meet and work with Mr. Mandela and connecting him with our production team. This was big! I had met President Mandela two years prior with a team from the Salvation Army, but this was going to be a special moment of working with him for a day. I was excited and nervous at the same time. Here was the man that was an icon for our nation and a global statesman working with us on the project about values.

I waited patiently by the door where he was going to come in to work with us. We had everything ready, the production crew was on standby, the cameras connected, the lights ready. Even though he was now well in his late 80's, he was still a very busy man and his time was precious. The security detail came in first and scoped the area and then without much warning, he appeared through the doorway with Zelda his personal assistant by his side. What immediately struck me was his height and his commanding presence and then his beaming smile!

Still smiling he greeted me "Oh young man, good to see you again!" I was completely caught off guard. It had been 2 years and I certainly did not expect him to remember me and besides I had been part of a team when I first met him. But here was this legend of our age, greeting little-old-me as an old friend. While I was still finding the right words to respond, he said "Do you remember me?" In my head, I was thinking 'You're Nelson Mandela! Of course, I remember you!' but I managed to say something that I can't even remember now.

Captured in that moment for me was the essence of this great man. Nelson Mandela lived his values and this was reflected in how he valued people. His security detail knew that whatever event they went to he would want to meet and shake the hands of the service people. Yes, the people who waited tables and cleaned the venue as well as the police. On stage, he connected with all the dignitaries but behind the scenes without the cameras he wanted to shake the hands of the people that did the work.

People respected Nelson Mandela not only because of the amazing things which he achieved in his lifetime, which were many, but because of the clarity of his values and principles.

Writing about Nelson Mandela, Richard Stengel in his book '*Nelson Mandela Portrait of An Extraordinary Man*' he says

'Nelson Mandela is a man of principle - exactly one: Equal rights for all, regardless of race, class or gender. Pretty much everything else is a tactic.'

This one principle shaped all his adult life and his other values emanated from it. When you are clear about what your values are, others don't have to guess what you stand for. But more importantly it becomes easier to make decisions about your everyday choices because the foundation is set. Leading a great life is about choosing to live based on your values, which in turn shapes your character and forms your reputation. Think about what you want to be known for, because therein lies your values.

Nobody but you can choose the values that guide your life. You already have values, most of them were formed in your childhood. Some of the values you have inherited are great and they have directed your life in the right direction, but some that you picked along the way can also be bad. To unleash your greatness, you need to become clear about what values you choose to live by and what values to let go of. Because, trust me what you value always shines through.

VALUES

6. Defining Your Values

"You'll look up and down streets. Look 'em over with care. About some you will say, "I don't choose to go there."

- Dr. Seuss (Oh the places you'll go)

Values can be a funny thing, we all have them, because we know that deep down some things are just right for us and some just aren't. But often when asked to define our values we find ourselves scrambling to find the right response. Why is that? Simple, we take our values for granted, we know they are there and somehow we think that's enough.

We take our values for granted until we are asked to compromise them. At that point something within us puts up a fight. We just know that we are not willing to go down some roads as Dr. Seuss puts it.

I believe that it is ultimately more powerful to have more clarity about what values shape your life. Here is a story of Eric Liddell who was an athlete during the 1924 Olympic Games in Paris. Eric had a difficult decision to make. He was scheduled to run his best event, the 100 meters, on a Sunday. But as a devout Christian, he objected to competing on a Sunday. To remain true to his principles he was willing to forfeit the chance to win. At the last moment, a teammate Harold Abrams, who was Jewish, switched events with Liddell. Liddell ran the

400 on Tuesday and Abrams ran the 100 on Sunday. Both men honored their faiths (Abrams celebrated the Jewish Sabbath on Saturday). And both won - even though not running in their best events. Abrams won gold. Liddell also came first while breaking the world record for 400 meters. (*Source: Total Quality Life - Stan Toler*)

Your beliefs play a key role in shaping your values.

> **"Your beliefs become your thoughts. Your thoughts become your words. Your words become your actions. Your actions become your habits. Your habits become your values. Your values become your destiny."**
> **- Mahatma Ghandi**

Many of us confuse beliefs with religion. Yes, religion and faith do play a big role in your belief system but you don't have to be religious to have beliefs. A belief defines an idea or principle which we judge to be true. We all have beliefs about all sorts of things, even if we cannot provide empirical evidence to support them. We have beliefs about people who live New York, Chicago or London. We have beliefs about the right way to raise our children. We have beliefs about gender roles in a marriage (and some of these can determine how long we remain married) and many more. Since we all have varying beliefs about different things based on where we were raised and what we were taught, we all have different values.

To unleash your greatness, you may want to evaluate your beliefs and ask yourself if those beliefs are in keeping with the person you want to be? The person you described in Section One. Can you Be Who You Be if you keep these beliefs or should you change?

Your values are determined by the standards you want to set for yourself and the things you are not willing to compromise on. To do great work and to live a great life you need to set standards that are in keeping with the level you want to reach. You might be reading this and think - yes I get it, but how do I go about it? I thought you would never ask!

Let me start by saying that you should listen to your inner voice more than what you think everybody expects of you.

There Is A Voice Inside Of You
That Whispers All Day Long
I Feel That This Is Right For Me
I Know That This Is Wrong
No Teacher, Preacher, Parent
Friend Or Wise Man Can Decide
What's Right For You - Just Listen To
The Voice That Speaks Inside
- Shel Silverstein

To help you along, let me share my personal core values that guide my decisions and my life. My core values should describe how I see myself and how I want others to see me.

I want to be known as a person of:

Humility - Approachable, respectful and willing to learn.

Authenticity - What you see is what you get, real and honest.

Influence - Inspiring, leading and a catalyst for change.

Love - Caring, compassionate and loyal.

Note that my Core Values also spell the acronym *HAIL*, which helps me with memorizing them. I believe that putting your own definition for what each of your core values means, also helps you personalize the values so they have a deeper meaning for you.

Now over to you! Without complicating this let's go through a few simple steps that will guide you through your own core values selection. Remember that you as an individual have many values but we want to focus on the four or five that you choose as the most important for the person you want to be. This is not a once off exercise, my hope is that you will do this again and again as you reach new stages in your life. Let's begin!

Identifying Your Core Values

STEP 1: Using a pencil, look through the list of core values in Table 1:1 and circle about 10 of your top values. These are the ones you feel best resonate with you. Feel free to add your own too.

STEP 2: Go through your list of the 10 words you selected and decide which of them are the ones that define what's most important to you. With a highlighter, highlight only 3 to 5 as your core values.

Authenticity	Balance	Compassion	Creativity
Achievement	Beauty	Challenge	Curiosity
Adventure	Boldness	Community	Determination
Authority		Competency	Duty
Autonomy		Contribution	Diligence
Fairness	Growth	Influence	Leadership
Faith	Happiness	Harmony	Learning
Friendship	Honesty	Justice	Love
Fun	Humor	Kindness	Loyalty
	Humility	Knowledge	Meaningful
Openness	Recognition	Security	Success
Optimism	Religion	Self-Respect	Status
Peace	Reputation	Service	Trustworthy
Pleasure	Responsibility	Spirituality	Wealth
Poise		Stability	Wisdom

Table 1:1 Common Core Values

Step 3: Write out your 3 to 5 core values in the spaces below:

My Core Values Are:

1...

2...

3...

4...

5...

Step 4: Write your values again and this time describe what they mean to you in the same fashion I did above.

My Core Values Meanings:

1...

2...

3...

4...

5...

Step 5: If possible try and arrange your values in a way that they create an acronym that will be your own personal values slogan.

You are now a proud owner of your own set of core values. To put your values into action, consider the decisions you must take this week and then weigh them against these and see which direction you will start moving.

BEHAVIOR

7. From Values To Action

"You cannot consistently perform in a manner which is inconsistent with the way you see yourself."

- Zig Ziglar

Unleashing your greatness calls on you to take responsibility for your actions and behaviors. You cannot continually blame your environment, your parents and your education for the way you are acting now. Unfortunately, too many people live their lives like this. You might have heard the following phrases from very capable people who keep making the same mistakes:

"It's not my fault that my relationships don't last because I have commitment issues"

"I can't seem to hold down a steady job, I always mess it up somehow"

I am sure you can add your own excuses to this list, but if you are to unleash your greatness you need to let go of those excuses and take full responsibility for your behaviors. Your behavior reveals what you truly believe. Adopting great core values should translate into great behavior that is consistent with those values. You need to watch your behavior and continually analyze what's influencing your decisions and actions.

The relationship between your values and your behaviors is like the iceberg that you find floating in the cold oceans.

You see an iceberg is an impressive thing to behold. Most icebergs are literary massive mountains of ice that break away from the arctic caps and float further away into warmer waters. If you were to see an iceberg while floating on small fisherman's boat it will loom high above your little boat. But no matter how high the part of the iceberg that you see, it's only about 10 percent of the total ice mass. 90 percent of the iceberg is below the water surface. The heavier and more dense ice is below the surface and it is what allows the iceberg to remain steady on the water.

Your behavior is like that top part of the iceberg, it's what everybody sees when they look at you. The dense 90 percent below the surface are your values and principles. The more refined, articulated and carefully applied those values are, the more refined and impressive the behavior gets. Show me someone who has an impressive, great behavior and I will show you someone who deeply understands and respects his/her core values. The opposite is true. Show me someone who is all over the place with erratic behavior and I will show you someone who is not in touch with his/her core values and who has no clear principles.

But we all have a choice.

Take some time and revisit your core values from the previous chapter. Look at each core value you selected and ask yourself the following questions:

What behaviors ought to be evident in my life if I live this value successfully?

How will this behavior affect those I regularly interact with?

What changes will be a result of these behaviors in my life?

As you go through each value separately and ask the three questions above you will hopefully start to see the correlation between your values, behavior and success. There is a direct line that connects your values to your current and future success but the only person that can connect those dots is you by choosing to live in the way that is consistent with your core values.

Most organizations now understand that there needs to be more than just values to create a right culture. These organizations are now putting more emphasis on communicating the kind of behaviors that are expected from their people.

The progression to unleashing greatness, which we have already followed in this book, is: First, clarify your identity, by clarifying what distinguishes you and having clear purpose or understanding your *Why*. Then get clear about what you stand for by defining your values and articulating the behaviors that shape your actions.

This is how great people and organizations set themselves apart and achieve great things as a result.

STRATEGY

8. Your Green Apron Book

"Successful people do what's right no matter how they feel about it. They don't expect to be able to feel their way into action. They act first...my values, not my feelings, need to control my actions"

- John C. Maxwell

If you want your values to impact your behavior, then you need to have a strategy to do it. Great leaders understand that it's not enough to communicate values but that you need to make them second nature to how things are done.

Great companies all over the world have one thing in common: A clearly articulated Values to Action Strategy.

Now think of yourself as a successful individual that delivers great results consistently in the way that you perform and live your life. What is that '*secret sauce*' that makes you deliver greatness time and time again? What strategy do you use to make sure that you always deliver based on your stated core values? What if you could come up with a clear answer to that? Well, now you can.

To do that, let's take this exercise out there on the road. Let's go to your local Starbucks, yes the one that you love going to. But as you go there I want you to do something for me. I want you to become observant as you interact with the staff and enjoy your beverage in one of those chairs or comfy sofas available. Take notice of the way you are greeted when you get to the counter. The way your order is taken and the way you receive it. Notice, that although the encounter is brief and to the point there is something to it. Try to get a handle on that. What is it that they do that others in the same industry don't?

Two things would have happened. One, you noticed the difference I am talking about, in the way you were served and the environment you enjoyed. Or, two, you are thinking what in the world am I going on about?

Let's start with a second response. It is possible that you are so used to this experience that it has become second nature for you. You don't see it as extraordinary because it's what you've come to expect. But, just imagine for a minute if any of what you take for granted was changed. If you don't get a courteous welcome when you get to the front of the line, instead a hazy look and a 'what do you want?' Would that bother you? What about if you felt that you were not welcome to stay but rather expected to move along after you got your coffee, would you notice then?

A core component of the Starbucks brand is "The Starbucks Experience." Going beyond commodity 'service' to deliver an experience.

In his book, **The Starbucks Experience: 5 Principles of turning ordinary into extraordinary**, Joseph Michelli shares components of what made Starbucks one of the growth stories of our time. His first principle from the Starbucks example is "Make It Your Own." Leadership encouraged the employees to "Make Starbucks their own" while providing the how-to-guide to make that happen. They didn't develop a huge complicated manual, instead, they created a simple small pocket book called '**The Green Apron Book**'.

The 'Green Apron Book' is exactly what it says, it's a small book that fits into the pocket of the green apron that employees wear every day at work. The book highlights that employees or 'partners' (as they are called) can merge the customer service objectives with their own personality and style. This makes sure that every day, they can fully be who they are while fully representing the brand. So instead of giving everyone a script that they need to follow, they provide behaviors that are expected.

Let me explain. Most companies will tell you how to answer the phone or greet the customer by giving you the exact words you must use, like "ABC incorporated, how can I help you?" The problem with this is that it's completely devoid of personality and connection. You might as well be talking to an answering machine. Not at Starbucks, employees can greet the way they want, as long as it is guided by the 5 behaviors in line with their values.

The Green Apron Book narrowed delivering 'Legendary Service' to five key behaviors:

1   **Be Welcoming,**
2   **Be Genuine**
3   **Be Knowledgeable,**
4   **Be Considerate, and**
5   **Be Involved.**

When a partner demonstrates these, they are doing the things that create the experience that keeps customers coming back. They are living the brand! This makes delivering 'Legendary Service' accessible and completely personal. It makes people feel that they are in charge of what they deliver while being authentic to the core values of the organization.

What about you? You can also narrow down your own behaviors based on your defined core values. You can create your very own 'Green Apron Book' as it were, that will massively impact your life and help you achieve greatness on your own terms. As a leader, you can also work with your team to turn your values into action by narrowing it down to a few behaviors.

You can do this no matter what field you work in. Whether working for yourself, and by yourself, leading a team of people in a department or running a massive operation you can create a strategy for living your values. Don't be tempted to complicate it. Keep it as simple as you can, besides we don't practice what we cannot remember. So, my suggestion for you is go back to your core values and turn them into behaviors that you can live and work by.

Here is what my 'Green Apron Book' strategy looks like:

As a professional speaker and consultant, I seek to inspire others to activate their potential. I am guided by the following behaviors:

- **Be Humble**
- **Be Authentic**
- **Be Influential**
- **Be Loving**

If I live and conduct myself in this way, I believe that I will attract the right customers and people into my life while being true to who I am and want to be.

Now that I have given you my template, go ahead and create your own simple strategy. Keep it simple and do it now.

Section 3: Pursue Excellence

The third key to unleashing your greatness is: Pursue Excellence!

"Excellence is doing ordinary things extraordinarily well."

- John W. Gardner

At the root of greatness is a continuous desire to pursue excellence, to do your best at being your best. I call it a pursuit of excellence because there cannot be a destination or a cap to what you can achieve. You cannot be great by settling for what is normal, comfortable or easy. Greatness requires from us a drive and a thirst to be better than our good. The reason we admire greatness in others is because we realize that it is not easily attained, nor handed to anyone on a platter.

Wealth and comfort can be passed down from one generation to another but greatness is an individual effort. For anyone who has ever been great at anything, no matter what profession or pursuit, has done so by attaining a level of excellence. In this section, we will look at key elements for pursuing excellence.

Buhle Dlamini

EXCELLENCE

9. Good Enough Is Not Good Enough

"If we did all the things we are capable of, we would literally astound ourselves."

- Thomas Edison

Have you ever said to yourself after working on something that it was good enough? 'Good enough' is a code for settling for less than what is possible. Good enough is throwing in the towel, giving in and resigning yourself to mediocrity. Pursuing excellence is about pushing beyond the levels where others settle.

Imagine you are a single young woman in search of a committed relationship with someone who could be your future husband. You sign up to an online dating site and create your profile, you spend time selecting the picture that best positions you and your best features. You write about your hobbies; you describe your dreams and favorite colors. As you work on your profile, you are careful to make sure that your potential suitors know that you are interested in a serious committed relationship. Now comes the section where you describe what you are looking for in a partner. Do you put 'I'm just looking for someone who's good enough'?

What? GOOD ENOUGH!

Of course, not! You are not looking for just Good Enough. You are looking for Mr. Right! You are looking for your proverbial Knight in Shining Armor! You describe the kind of traits you want in a man and you are not looking for a compromise and you aim as high as you can. But you don't settle for just Good Enough!

> "Shoot for the moon. Even if you miss, you'll land among the stars." - Norman Vincent Peale

In my presentations, I often ask my audience to repeat this phrase aloud:

GOOD ENOUGH IS NOT GOOD ENOUGH!

Too many of us settle for less than we are capable of having, doing and being. You will hardly ever have more than what you are willing to settle for. You will definitely never do more than what you are willing to settle for. And you will never become more than what you are willing to settle for.

You only rise to the level you settle for!

Tony Robbins often shares a great story of how a homeless man once asked him for a quarter. He stopped, looked at the homeless man, opened his wallet, and exposed ten, twenty and even hundred dollar bills in his wallet and pulled out the quarter for the man. He made sure that the man was aware that he had much more money, and asked him "Are you sure you only want a quarter?" The man replied "Yes can I have a quarter please?" He gave the man the quarter and said, "Life pays you the price you ask for." The man looked at Tony, the quarter, the wallet filled with bills and took the quarter saying, *"You are weird!"* That story always makes me chuckle.

Remember, 'Life Will Pay Whatever Price You Ask For'. Nothing more, nothing less! So, what is it that you are asking for? What is it that you really want for yourself? If it is greatness, then you need to stop settling and start reaching. Stop playing small and start going for the big league. This decision changes everything, because you will start expecting more of yourself and demanding more for yourself. So, I repeat, Good Enough Is Not Good Enough!

Disney released a powerful movie in 2016 called 'The Queen of Katwe'. It is based on the vibrant true story of a young girl from an impoverished slum in Uganda. For 10-year-old Phiona Mutesi (acted by Madina Nalwanga) and her family, life in the impoverished slum of Katwe in Kampala, is a constant struggle. They live a life of survival with her siblings and their single widowed mother (Lupita Nyong'o). Phiona's world rapidly changes when she is introduced to the game of chess by a committed coach Robert Katende (David Oyelowo).

Coach Katende immediately notices that Phiona is kind of a chess prodigy, even without a day of schooling in her life she masters the game in no time. This brings her to a whole new world of possibility as she enters tournaments in faraway amazing places, even though she still had to return to the struggle that is her life in Katwe. At a key moment Phiona feels that there is no point in pushing for more than what she is. She says to her coach in resignation, "what's the point coach? I am just a girl from Katwe, all I know is selling maze for a living, I cannot be a chess master!"

Coach Robert Katende responds with these powerful words:

"Sometimes the place you are used to, is not where you belong. You belong where you believe you belong. Where is that for you?"

I turn the question over to you. Where do you think you belong? Do you believe that there is more for you than what you are settling for? If so, decide now that you will no longer settle for just Good Enough. Decide to push yourself with every effort, every project and every dream you have not to settle for just good enough.

In what areas, have you settled for Good Enough?

Take some time and list them and resolve to change.

EFFORT

10. Put The Extra To Your Ordinary

"Playing with Michael Jordan on the Olympic team, there was a huge gap between his ability and the ability of other great players on the Olympic team. But what impressed me was that he was always the first one on the floor and the last one to leave."

- Steve Alford

Excellence takes effort! What you put in is what you get out. More often than not, the one thing that makes the great among us better than most, is the effort they put in. Talent is important. But talent alone does not guarantee success and greatness. All over the world people with more talent on their pinky finger, work for people with much less talent who are willing to put in the effort that is required for them to be the best in their field.

Think back to high school, picture some of the kids that had incredible talent, the ones that everybody said were most likely to succeed. How many of them have met the expectations that people had for them? Can you think of some, who inspite of having everything they needed to succeed ended up being huge disappointments? That is because talent alone is not enough. If you want to unleash your greatness, no matter who you are and what you have, you need to put extra effort to excel.

Put More Effort Than What Others Are Willing To.

The Ritz Carlton Hotel brand is synonymous with quality and excellence. As a matter of fact, when people want to describe something as the pinnacle of its field they refer to it as 'The Ritz Carlton of that industry" Why? The answer lies in this brand's commitment to putting in more effort than what the rest are willing to. The Ritz Carlton gives its Ladies and Gentlemen (they don't refer to them as staff) a daily budget they can spend at their discretion for every customer. This means for example, that a bell boy can decide to purchase shaving cream for a customer who realizes they forgot to bring some, at the Hotel's expense! Yes, you got that right, they are encouraged to go out of their way to make sure that the customer is as satisfied as possible.

The culture of extra effort is part of the whole experience when you stay at one of their hotels anywhere in the world. Nothing is too much for the 'Ladies and Gentlemen' of the Ritz. This is the reason that discerning customers are willing to pay so much more to stay at the Ritz. It's not just for the amazing furniture, exquisite food and comfortable beds that the customers want to stay there, it is for the total attention to detail they experience.

To unleash your greatness, you need to commit yourself to having this attitude and ethic to the work you do. The willingness to put that extra effort than what is expected. The reason we notice and tip more for good service is because we recognize the value that extra effort plays in giving us a great experience. The same applies to everything else. Excellence demands reciprocity.

> **"It's never crowded along the extra mile" - Dr. Wayne W. Dyer**

Wayne Dyer nailed it on the head when he said "It's never crowded along the extra mile." To be on the league of your own, you need to embrace the extra mile mindset and make it a core part of the way you do things and operate. I often tell my audiences that if they want to see great results they need to ask themselves how much extra effort they are willing to make to make it happen. Like Michael Jordan was always the first one on the floor and the last one to leave, we need to be willing to go the required extra mile in our field.

If you deal with customers on an ongoing basis consider taking some time preparing for each meeting you have with them. Learn their name and even how to pronounce it properly before you meet them. Take the time to research some of their previous work or current involvement to show them you are interested in them as much as you are interested in their business. You will be amazed at how much a little personal touch does to create a successful transaction.

When organizations invite me to speak at their staff conferences, they are often amazed to see me going through the crowd before my talk and meeting people as they come in. During this time, I ask people who they are and do my best to remember their names. I also ask them what they do and what projects they are working on. This simple exercise alone increases my connection with my audiences that results in standing ovations.

As I deliver my speech after having worked the room, I am no longer talking to strangers but friends and I bring them in to my examples. Imagine the surprise as Sue from HR on row F hears me reference her by name in my speech as I talk about the project she's working on to make a point. I do this over and over, that it has become part of my 'modus operandi'. It is not expected of me and it is not common in my field, as most speakers treat themselves as big-time celebrities and often making ridiculous demands of their clients. I have heard of speakers who demand M&M's in their 'green room' and only want the yellow or green ones separated.

I choose to be different. I choose to go the extra mile for my clients and as result they recommend me to others.

COMMITMENT

11. Take Full Ownership

"The quality of a person's life is in direct proportion to their commitment to excellence, regardless of their chosen field of endeavor."

- Vince Lombardi

'It's not part of my job description' is one of the most repeated phrase that managers and supervisors often hear in the workplace. Most people live and work from the principle of doing no more than what is expected of them.

A picture that made rounds on the internet is one of a flat small wild animal in the middle of a street that had been run over by traffic and right over it is a freshly painted yellow middle line. The caption that goes with it - Winner of It's Not My Job Award!

This image, while it is quite funny, is also quite sad because it describes so many people who do not take ownership for what they do and where they are going. And it is not as uncommon as we might think. People go to work daily in companies, schools, and government with this attitude. They don't take ownership of the work they do and they couldn't care less about what the consequences are.

Maybe you are one of those people. Maybe you are fed up with your company, your manager or your team. Well, if you don't love it and can't take pride in the work you do then consider changing jobs. Seriously, maybe you should fire your company or your boss in search of work that will have meaning for you and demand your commitment. You will never reach your full potential without having commitment and ownership of what you do. Don't fool yourself by saying that 'at least it pays the bills!' Do you real want to be the winner of 'It's Not My Job Award?'

> **"You must take personal responsibility. You cannot change the circumstances, the seasons, or the wind, but you can change yourself." - Jim Rhohn**

I recently had an opportunity to share a convention stage with Jack Canfield, the co-author of *Chicken Soup for The Soul* series. In one of Jack's best-selling books' *The Success Principles* he says:

"One of the most pervasive myths in the American culture today is that we are entitled to a great life - that somehow, somewhere, someone (certainly not us) is responsible for filling our lives with continual happiness, exciting career options, nurturing family time, and blissful personal relationships simply because we exist. But the truth is that there is only one person responsible for the quality of the life you live. That person is you."

I couldn't have said it better. To get a quality life you must take personal responsibility to make it so. But let me take it one step further, if you want your work to be fulfilling you need to take ownership. As long as you place ownership of what you do on someone else's hands greatness will elude you.

So, excellence requires you to take personal ownership of everything you do. Choose to adopt the slogan "If it is to be it is up to me!"

What does taking personal ownership look like for you?

LEGACY

12. What Are You Building?

"We are what we repeatedly do. Excellence then is not an act but a habit"

- Aristotle

The story has been told many times in many ways and it's a story of the most acclaimed architect, Sir Christopher Wren and the interaction he had with the builders at the building site of London's St Paul's Cathedral. Wren, who was not personally known by the many workers at the site of the Cathedral he had designed, visited the site one day. He stopped and engaged three laborers who were busy working there, on the same task. He asked them what they were doing? He got three different answers.

The first man said, "I am cutting this stone."

The second man said, "I am earning three shillings, six pence a day."

The third man straightened up, squared his shoulders, and still holding his mallet and chisel, replied, "I am helping Sir Christopher Wren build this great cathedral."

Not even knowing he was addressing Sir Christopher Wren himself, this man made a massive impact on the great architect that he shared his story that has been passed on till today.

Three men working on the same task but only one of them understood the great key to excellence and greatness is to be willing to work for a cause greater than yourself. No matter what work you end up doing if you choose to build a legacy of excellence then greatness will follow.

Unfortunately, the world is filled with people just like the first two laborers, people who do tasks in a meaningless way and those that only work for a living. Both approaches cannot lead to personal fulfilment on the part of the individual, nor excellence in the way the work is done.

Pursuing excellence requires us to be completely engaged and captured by the vision of the work we are involved in. If I only speak because somebody needs a speaker to fill a slot at a conference, my efforts will reflect this and I will make little or no impact. On the same token if I only speak because I am going to get paid, my efforts will be determined by the size of the payment I expect to receive. Both are very poor substitutes for excellence.

The reason I get up to speak, whether to a small group of high schoolers or to senior executives at a glitzy convention center, is for the opportunity to inspire my audience to activate their potential. See how my *purpose* gives a compelling reason to excel and be the best I can be? Like the inspired laborer, I am driven to produce my best work by this grand vision; that what I am doing will leave a legacy long after the lights have dimmed.

> **"Quality is never an accident; it is always the result of high intention, sincere effort, intelligent direction, and skillful execution; it represents the wise choice of many alternatives." - William A. Forster**

To become all we can be, we need to be driven by a greater vision, that the way we live and the labor we put in today, will leave a legacy. Your legacy is what builds your reputation. The more you deliver excellence, the more your reputation grows and your legacy starts to speak for itself. The best way to secure your future is to do your work of today in such a way that people start promoting you without you asking them.

Pursuing excellence and greatness is about setting your own standard and not merely measuring up to accepted standards. It is about deciding that something more than average is what you are capable of and expected to achieve, because you can!

Tom Peters challenges us in this way:

"Think Excellence
Don't cut corners!
Think Excellence
Care more than others think is wise!
Think Excellence
Dream more than others think is practical!
Think Excellence
Expect more than others think is possible!"

Buhle Dlamini

Section 4: Unleash A Winning Attitude

The fourth key to unleashing your greatness is: Unleash A Winning Attitude!

"Your living is determined not so much by what life brings to you as by the attitude you bring to life; not so much by what happens to you as by the way your mind looks at what happens."
- Khalil Gibran

Attitude affects everything! The way you see the world has more to do with your attitude than it has to do with the world itself. Ever noticed how people from the same family can have totally different dispositions even though they eat the same food and live under the same roof? The answer to the differing dispositions lies in the way they see the world. Their attitude!

Attitude is a big part of unleashing your greatness because it determines the way you see the world, which in turn affects how you perform in that world. You will never find a person who has amassed great success in any field without a winning attitude. Attitude is essential because you cannot control the events that will happen to you in the world but with a great attitude you will be able to control how you respond to those events.

Buhle Dlamini

ATTITUDE

13. How You Show Up

"Sooner or later, those who win are those who think they can."

- Richard Bach

Winners understand that the inward battle is much more important than the battle out there. What you believe about yourself and the world around you ultimately determines how you perform.

What every athlete knows is that it doesn't matter how well prepared you are physically, or how much energy you have, if your attitude doesn't say win, you will not win. If you step onto the plate and get intimidated by the size of your opponent and start having doubts about your own ability, your own performance becomes affected by how you show up.

Your Attitude Determines Your Approach to Work and Life

How you show up affects everything. Your attitude tells you what to expect from life, if you expect great things to happen, you are drawn to great opportunities, if you expect everything to be hard, you're drawn to the problems in your life. It all begins with the way you see the world.

A story is told about a Grandpa who was taking a nap on his chair in the lounge one afternoon. Realizing that their Grandpa was fast asleep, his grandchildren decided to play a trick on him. They got from the pantry a piece of very stinky cheese and put it on his moustache. The stench of the cheese soon woke him up. As he was sniffing, he exclaimed, "This room stinks!" and got up to move to the kitchen. As soon as he got to the kitchen he sniffed again and said, "It stinks here too!" so he walked out the back door into the garden. Much to his surprise, the smell was there too, and he proclaimed, "The whole world stinks!"

Makes you think about how we often live our lives. If we are carrying stinky cheese in our attitudes it doesn't matter what the world throws at us it will all stink.

According to John C. Maxwell in his book *The Winning Attitude* - "Our attitude determines our approach to life." Our attitude can determine whether we see ourselves as prisoners to our circumstances or victors. He says, "Sometimes the prison of discontent has been built by our own hands." How true and challenging that view is! Your victory or defeat is determined by the lenses with which you choose to see your world.

To unleash your greatness, you need to choose to unleash a winning attitude. You need to choose what attitude governs your life and actions. This is one area you cannot delegate to others.

So, what is this thing we call attitude?

> **"Attitude is an inward feeling expressed by behavior." – John C. Maxwell**

Attitude is as much about choice as it is about feelings. Feelings come and go but attitude is a determined way to look at things. We all have feelings, that's what makes us human. We sometimes feel sad, happy, excited or fearful based on what we are going through. We are not confined by these feelings, because as real as they are, so is our ability to change them. The only way to do this is by focusing on what our beliefs are. What you believe about yourself and your situation is what ultimately shapes your attitude.

YES WE CAN!

In 2008 a political campaign took the world by storm. It was by a young black Senator from Illinois, Barrack Obama, who was running for the highest office in the United States of America. Everything said it couldn't be done. The history of racial discrimination and political tensions said it couldn't be done. Even many people of color in the US said it couldn't be done. But all of that was before they experienced something refreshing that was to sweep throughout the country because of this one candidate. The attitude of possibility was encompassed by his central message of 'Yes We Can!'

It started as rumblings of possibility but it quickly became a rushing movement of 'change in our lifetime!' None of it would have been possible without a winning attitude of a passionate man with a strong belief that America could rise to fulfil it's true calling as a beacon of hope for all races.

His winning attitude was relentless as opponents from within his own party and from the opposition did their best to ridicule his attempt and belief that he can be President. His attitude soon became contagious as he moved from state to state and calling others to believe with him. The chanting of 'Yes We Can' did something more powerful than motivating his base, it changed the very atmosphere to become charged with possibility.

This is the very reason that athletes who repeat positive statements to themselves about their ability to win, actually end up winning. A winning attitude is about talking yourself into winning. It is about silencing the negative voice inside you that is constantly trying to tell you that you can't.

So, the challenge for you on this journey to greatness is: change your beliefs about what you can achieve. You have to change what you believe about your environment so that you can see the opportunities that it holds. You have to decide that you are more than a conqueror and that your best days are still ahead of you not behind you. You must draw a line in the sand and proclaim about your future - YES I CAN!

So, if you want to know what is the secret ingredient for winners in our world? It is simply this: choosing an attitude that believes in the possibility of winning no matter the odds.

Like Barack Obama did in 2008, we must silence our own cynics and our own critics.

> **"We are the hope of the future; the answer to the cynics who tell us our house must stand divided; that we cannot come together; that we cannot remake this world as it should be...Yes We Can"**
>
> **– Barack Obama, Super Tuesday Feb 2008**

A winning attitude refuses to be confined by how the world is but chooses to embrace how the world could be. With your attitude, you can change the way you look at your work. With your attitude, you can replace the stinky cheese with a fresh perspective of possibility.

Right now, think about some of the negative views about your work, your industry and people that are holding you back. Now, decide to turn all those views on their head and choose to look at them differently. This won't magically change a negative situation into a positive one but it will change your approach in dealing with it.

Change the way you show up to work and you will change the way you work.

CHOICE

14. Thermometer or Thermostat?

"You may shoot me with your words,
You may cut me with your eyes,
You may kill me with your hatefulness,
But still, like air, I'll rise."

- Maya Angelou

Nothing is as powerful as choice. But powerful still is seeing someone who uses their choice. This is what a winning attitude is all about. At the root of a winning attitude is your willingness to choose your response to whatever is thrown at you.

Viktor Frankl was one of the survivors of the horrendous experience of Nazi Germany's concentration camps. Nothing can describe the desperate situation that he and many other Jews suffered at these camps, save to say that for many, death would have been a welcome relief. Viktor, captures what made the difference for some who chose to look at their situation differently. He writes:

"We who lived in concentration camps can remember the men who walked through the huts comforting others, giving away their last piece of bread. They may have been few in number, but they offer sufficient proof that everything can be taken from a man but one thing: *the last of the human freedoms—to choose one's attitude in any given set of circumstances, to choose one's own way.*

And there were always choices to make. Every day, every hour, offered the opportunity to make a decision, a decision which determined whether you would or would not submit to those powers which threatened to rob you of your very self, your inner freedom; which determined whether or not you would become the plaything of circumstance, renouncing freedom and dignity to become molded into the form of the typical inmate." (Viktor Frankl, abridged and adapted from, *"Man's Search for Meaning"*)

I continue to find these words challenging as I look at my own life. Do I appreciate the choice I have every day in deciding who I am going to be and how I am going to be? Because ultimately this power lies with me.

Let me tell you about the change that took place in my own life not long ago. My wife, Stacey, is from Canada in the province of Nova Scotia on the east coast. We met in our teen years in 1997, when she came to South Africa to a youth conference and we connected. In 2002 we got married after a five-year long-distance relationship and she moved to South Africa. We lived in Johannesburg for the years that followed until 2013 when we decided to move to Canada for several years to be closer to her family.

We arrived in Canada in December, to start our new life with our children. It was DECEMBER! And that year the snow came early. On the second week of December there was already 25cm of snow and I thought to myself, "What have I come to?" In the months that followed the brutality of the Canadian winter hit me like a ton of bricks. Not only was it cold but the lovely house we had bought was massive and an old oil guzzler for heating. Imagine my shock the first time I saw the heating oil truck pull over in front of the house and offloading hundreds of liters of oil to keep the house warm. Then came the bill that made this grown man cry.

Dealing With Change

I had made every single major change that most adults go through, except having a new baby. I moved to a new country where people couldn't even say my name. I moved into a new home in a totally different climate and I was starting a new business! I was dealing with massive changes all at once. But I was determined that I was not going to fail. I decided in my heart and spirit that I was going to succeed, even though it seemed that all the odds were against me.

Soon after, in the middle of the winter my dining room ceiling started to leak, a result of too much snow that was collecting on the roof and making its way under roof tiles/shingles. I was told that I needed a roof rake to remove the snow from my roof. What the heck was a *roof rake*? In South Africa, we used the rakes for leaves in our gardens, where had I come to? So, I bought myself a roof rake and in the middle of a cold February morning, there I was knee deep in snow with a long inverted rake trying to remove snow from my roof.

This scene must have caused a bit of a stir in our small town of Pictou (population - 4000, black families - 1.5, I think) because a steady stream of slow moving cars started to cause a traffic jam in our quiet street.

In all this change, I learned a valuable lesson. My house has a thermostat in every room to regulate how much heat each room gets. This helps, when we are downstairs during the day we turn the heat low upstairs where the bedrooms are and vice versa. This helped me to understand something about attitude.

Attitude is the internal thermostat that controls your internal condition which affects your output!

What a revelation this was for me! I had a choice, to be a thermometer merely reflecting the conditions around me. Or I could choose to be a thermostat and control my response to whatever condition I find myself in. I chose to be a thermostat and let a winning attitude guide my approach to life.

Did this stop the challenges I faced? Of course, not! But attitude greatly affected how I responded to those challenges. Even as I was fighting for survival for my business in South Africa and starting a new business in Canada. I decided I was going to win! I decided that I was not going to give up and blame my circumstances. So, I got to work on my challenges, I figured out solutions and used what I had to get what I needed. This ability to choose my own response to situations that I face has been my key to success.

You can do the same. Choose to be a thermostat and not merely a thermometer. Stop reflecting what's around you and begin to shape your environment. Your attitude will become a huge weapon in your arsenal, start using it.

"There's A Little Difference Between People But That Little Difference Makes A Big Difference And That Difference Is ATTITUDE"
– John C. Maxwell

Some professional drivers "go to work" every morning, while others "go for a drive in the country side" it all depends on how you see it. If you want to unleash your greatness, choose a great attitude.

What winning attitudes will shape your life?

Write some of them below:

....
....
....
....

Examples: Optimism, Gratitude, Determination, Helpfulness, Hopefulness, Courage, Self-confidence, Tolerance and Self-discipline.

BELIEF

15. You Have What It Takes

"Everything you need you already have. You are complete right now; you are a whole, total person, not an apprentice person on the way to someplace else. Your completeness must be understood by you and experienced in your thoughts as your own personal reality."

- Sarah Ban Brethnach, (Simple Abundance)

The last aspect of having a great attitude is believing in yourself and accepting yourself as the winner that you are. A traveler came into a tattoo shop run by an old Chinese man. On the wall were lots of tattoo slogans that one could choose from. Many of these slogans were positive and sentimental but there were also some dark ones on display. The traveler's attention was caught by one tattoo that simply read 'LOSER', perplexed the traveler asked the old man, "who could ever engrave such a statement on their body permanently." The old man looked at the traveler and said, "Before tattoo on body, tattoo on mind!"

What you believe about yourself will manifest itself in your attitude which in turn becomes your actions.

On our journey to a fulfilled life we need to realize that we already have everything we need to live the life we were meant to live. I love the saying 'God don't make no junk' – when you were created, nothing was left out, you were given all that you would need for your life to be whole. You might not have what the next person has in terms of looks, skills and personality but for you it is what you need to be truly yourself.

Often we live our lives as if we're on our way to somewhere else, that someday in the future we will truly be whole. We can spend our whole lives in anticipation of what's next or we can choose to believe that we already have everything we need to have a full life now.

This also stops us from making excuses about what we can or cannot do. If you were meant to do something or to be somebody, then you already have what you need to be just that. The sooner you realize this, the sooner you start doing what you need to do to live out your true calling and as you go on that journey, things fall into place.

My Victory Begins the Moment I Believe That I Have What It Takes, That I Am Enough.

> **"Our duty, as men and women, is to proceed as if limits to our ability did not exist. We are collaborators in creation."**
>
> **- Pierre Teilhard de Chardin**

Believing in yourself is not just about sense of self-importance or arrogance, it is about embracing who you are and can be. It is deciding that you will no longer make excuses for yourself but you will go out and use what you already have been given to have a full life.

I love the story of the famous motivational speaker Les Brown, he struggled in school and was told at the young age that he was Educable Mentally Retarded. One day his teacher told him to go to the board and finish a sum. Les, said that he couldn't do it. The teacher asked him why? And his response was, "because I am Educable Mentally Retarded sir." The teacher looked him in the eye and said:

"Don't let someone else's opinion of you become your reality!"

Decide to get rid of any self-limiting beliefs you might have about yourself and stand tall because you are enough. Believe in yourself and your ability to create a great life. Believe that you can attempt the great things you sometimes find yourself doubting. And go make it happen!

Believing in yourself is the best attitude you can adopt to unleash your greatness.

Unleashing a winning attitude is about:

Deciding How You Show,

Choosing to Be a Thermostat, and

Believing in Yourself!

GRIT

16. Get Up After Failure

"I've missed more than 9000 shots in my career. I've lost almost 300 games. 26 times, I've been trusted to take the game winning shot and missed. I've failed over and over and over again in my life. And that is why I succeed."

\- Michael Jordan

'Never Give Up!' Is a phrase that is often linked to the attitude of winners and with good reason. Winners understand that in order to win, you've got to be willing to fail, a lot! If you fear failure then you will never be a winner, period! A winning attitude accepts the very plausible chance of failing on your journey to success, and deciding to go ahead and try anyway.

One of Nike's campaigns is Finding Your Greatness and in one of the ads it portrays numerous ordinary young athletes in different locations across the world, it ends with a young man atop a very high diving board. You can almost feel the tension he feels standing at the edge of a great opportunity or a great disaster. In the ad, the narrator then says these words:

"Greatness is wherever somebody is trying to find it!"

Inspiring, goose-bumpy kind of stuff! But as an entrepreneur I know that feeling too well, having stood at the precipice of an opportunity that can either make you or break you. Many a time as business leaders we walk away after assessing the risks and decide that this is not for us, but more often than not we take the plunge. You see as entrepreneurs we are the plunge-takers; besides we took a plunge to start our own business or to run an organization even if we didn't start it ourselves.

The more we do it the easier it gets, until Dah, Dah, Daaah! We take a plunge that absolutely knocks the stuffing right out of us and leaves us dazed and confused. We bite more than we can chew at that time and then failure is not just a possibility but a reality. Have you ever attempted something so big that it would either bring you great success or great defeat? Have you found yourself at an end of a project that was meant to set you up for the big time, only to be worse than where you started? Well I have, and you probably have too, if not yet, trust me on your journey to greatness failure will come!

In 2014, I faced one of my biggest failures in business after having taken a bold move to 'go big or go home'. I went big and I almost went bust! I was shaken to the core. After years of positive trajectory in my business, here I was trying to grow businesses on two continents. The near failure, did not bring me down but I was shaken. Throughout this period, I was left asking questions like "what was I thinking?" "what did we do wrong?" "should we have done any of this?"

To be great you have to be willing to fail your way to success. You have to have the attitude of **GRIT** – that ability to stick with and pursue a goal even in the face of incredible odds. You will face failure or challenges along the way that will make you question yourself and your ability to succeed. But, you can find greatness beyond failure. Here is what I learned about finding greatness beyond my own failure:

Better to Risk Something and Fail Than to Risk Nothing

In business success is addictive and if you have been successful it is easier to take it for granted. And sometimes in our success, we get into maintenance mode, where we dare not risk messing with what we've got going on. This is where success becomes your enemy, you no longer try new things and you just protect what you have, even as it shrinks ever so slowly right in front of you.

When we take the necessary risks for our businesses and careers to grow we learn valuable lessons in the process as we are inevitably pushed into unfamiliar territory where we need to learn to sink or swim. Here and only here you earn your masters from the 'school-of-hard-knocks' as you have to negotiate, beg and become really humble really fast. It is also here that you appreciate real and true friends and clients who will stick with you through the rough times. When you take a risk, and fall, the off-shoot of that is that you learn a valuable lesson and healthy respect for gravity! I have become more calculated in the risks I take than before this experience. Will I take risks in the future? Absolutely! But I am so much wiser having taken one that hit me hard.

Don't Throw in The Towel Too Early

There will be many times where you will feel like: what's the point let me just give up, all is lost. But from personal experience, my advice to you is to keep going and not give in. Your biggest challenge here will be the knock to your self-confidence. After years of growing and winning victories here and there, you experience the excruciating pain of helplessness and it stings like hell. Most of the battle at this stage is an internal one and all the motivational books and videos don't seem to work. You feel like you are alone in the world. But...

you are not alone. There are people in your life who will be more than willing to walk the road with you. Just find them and connect with them.

Don't close the doors and fire your staff. Dig deeper than you've ever had to before and keep absolute defeat at arm's length, even when you know it hasn't left you, keep pushing back. Tell yourself repeatedly "this is going to pass, it has to, even if there is damage, I will not be destroyed by this."

Hope is Not a Strategy, Explore All Your Options

In your time of challenge, you will begin hoping and believing that you have a chance at winning the lottery, or that a venture capitalist is going to find you and call you to relieve you of your troubles. This is the hope instinct that we have as entrepreneurs and starters, the belief that things will work out. As the young Indian entrepreneur Sonny in the Best Exotic Marigold Hotel says:

> **"Everything will be all right in the end... if it's not alright then it's not yet the end."– Sonny (Best Exotic Marigold Hotel)**

It's a lovely sentiment but, hope is not a strategy. You need to put on your strategic hat and take the time to list all your options, even the ones that make your stomach turn, write them all down. Then put them in the order of preference starting with the easy wins and working your way to the absolute gut-wrenching actions you might have to take to get yourself back above the water.

Be Honest with Yourself but Don't Stop Believing in Yourself

Over the years, you have listened to and embraced the hype about yourself and your business or career success. This has given you a sense of self-worth and value and you started believing your own hype. Facing failure and a challenge can knock a lot of your self-worth and make you feel like a failure. The trick here, is to take it on the chin and be honest with yourself about your abilities and shortcomings but don't let it defeat you.

You are still the same guy or gal that had the guts to start something from nothing. You created value for your clients, provided employment for your team and provided for your family. You can still do this, in fact, your greatest success lies beyond your failure but in order to reach it you have to pass this test. Stop feeling sorry for yourself, nobody wants to hear your sob story. Don't tell everybody about your challenge, only the ones you can trust and who will help you through it.

Dig deep within yourself and summon that great warrior that is still able to dream even bigger dreams but only now you have wisdom that only comes from this side of failure. Remember Michael Jordan's famous quote:

> **"I have failed over and over again in my life .... and that is why I succeed." - Michael Jordan**

There is greatness beyond business and career failure but that is all up to you. All successful people have experienced failure more than once in their business or professional journey and what truly makes them great is their ability to rise above failure and reach greatness. You can do it too take it from me, I am doing it! Will you?

Section 5: Create Your Future

The fifth key to unleashing your greatness is: Create Your Future!

"Your future is created by what you do today, not tomorrow."

- Robert Kiyosaki

I have long learned that it is not our conditions that determine our future but the choices we make today. Unleashing your greatness requires you to be an active participant in creating your own future. You cannot let your fate be determined by chance, you must get up and do what you need to do, to make things happen.

When I look back at all my achievements, I am grateful for the opportunities I have had. But I also realize that the actions I took always brought me closer to being ready to grab those opportunities.

Never underestimate the power of a dream and action. When you take action today, you open doors for what *could* be tomorrow. Your greatest challenge to unleashing your greatness is accepting the responsibility to create your own future. The great future that awaits you, will require you to do something now and it will cost you.

Are you willing to pay the price for the great future you want?

VISION

17. Dare to Dream Big

"There is nothing like a dream to create the future."

- Victor Hugo

Let me start by saying that today I get to live in a home I could only dream of as a child. Not only that, I now own two homes on two continents that are both my home. I get to travel between my two countries (Canada and South Africa) regularly, as well as going to work in many other countries around the world. The life that I live now was once a dream that seemed as far away as the moon. But today those dreams are now my reality. Today, I am dreaming even bigger and bolder dreams for the future I want to have tomorrow.

I tell you this, not to brag about my life, but rather to illustrate that unleashing greatness is a reality for all of us because all of us can dream. Does this mean I don't have any challenges today? Not by a long shot! The challenges I now face, match the level that my life has risen to and so it is with all of us.

Everybody has a dream inside of them just waiting to be unleashed. But life has a way of beating dreams out of us. Well-meaning people like our parents and friends say things like, "You cannot build your life on dreams" and "stop being a dreamer and get real!" And after years of hearing these messages we start to internalize them and start thinking "Who am I to dream of such things anyway?" We silence our dreams and with that our potential for greatness.

> **"The greatest danger for most of us is not that our aim is too high and we miss it, but that it is too low and we reach it."**
>
> **-Michelangelo**

You need to get back in touch with your dreams. You know, the stuff you used to daydream about, the things you thought you can do and become. You still can! You still can be that person you imagined. Sure, some dreams have a deadline, as in most sports if you haven't started by a certain age there is a limit to what you can achieve. But dreams are not limited to a stage of your life. I truly believe that there is a dream for every stage of every person's life.

Some dream of travelling to places they read about in their youth, while others dream about getting that post-grad diploma, still others are dreaming about making a difference helping the less fortunate in their own city. That is what is cool about dreams, the only limit is your imagination. If you dare to attempt something that you know you can achieve, there is no telling how far you can go until you do it!

> **"The future belongs to those who believe in the beauty of their dreams."**
>
> **-Eleanor Roosevelt**

Now I invite you to tap into your dreams again. Take some time right now and think about the things you wanted to do with your life. I am not talking about your dreams to marry a member of the Royal Family or a Hollywood pop star. Although these can still happen, I want you to think about the kind of dreams that depend upon what you can do to make them happen. The dreams that unleash our greatness begin at end of our own arm, they are in our hands.

As I mentioned briefly, the life I get to live today is in direct correlation to the dreams I had for myself. I dreamed my current reality into being. This might sound a little strange or even ludicrous, but we attract what we dream and work towards, that's how life works. That which you focus on and work towards becomes your reality. If you change your focus and redirect your actions, your life changes as a result. No magic required!

That which you focus on and work towards becomes your reality.

How to Unleash the Power of Your Dreams?

1. Be Clear About What You Want

You need to get specific about your dreams. Clearly articulate what you want to achieve. Think about the size, the value and the details of your dream. Think about the impact your dream will have in your life, your family and others. You know how you know that it's a dream? If you get excited thinking about it, then it's a dream. If it pulls you forward and calls you higher, then it's a dream.

To help you clarify what you want, complete the following statements:

I am passionate about . . . .

. . . .

I want to make a difference in . . . .

. . . .

Success for me means . . . .

. . . .

2. Break Your Dreams into Categories

Now that you have some clarity about what you want for your life; break your dreams into specific categories. It is very important to know exactly what dreams you have for the different sections of your life. The dream you have professionally can affect the dream you have for your family being achieved. But when you have taken the time to have your dreams laid out you can then have dreams that complement each other.

Some people have a professional dream of being a jet setting corporate executive for a big company, while having a dream of having a life that allows them to spend a lot of time with their young family. The likelihood of both dreams being achieved at the same time is slim and so they should re-evaluate their dreams. This only happens when they are written down.

To help you categorize your dreams complete the following statements and try to be as specific as possible:

My Professional/Career/Financial Dream is…….……….....

……………………………………………………………………....

……………………………………………………………………....

My Personal/Family/Life Dream is………...………………....

……………………………………………………………………....

……………………………………………………………………....

My Contribution/Service/Impact Dream is………………….

……………………………………………………………………....

……………………………………………………………………....

Take all the time you need in doing this, go to a quiet spot somewhere you will not be disturbed and get in touch with your dreams.

3. Review, Clarify and Refine Your Dreams

Now that you have done the work of clarifying what you want out of your life and have written down specific dreams you want to chase in different parts of your life, take the time to review. Take the time to go over what you wrote, if needed find clearer and more descriptive words to define what you mean.

Don't be like the person who said, "I always wanted to be somebody, I wish I had been more specific." If you don't clarify for yourself where you want to be, you will find that years from now you're still in the same place.

After reviewing your dreams, you can rewrite them below and then, transfer them to a place you can see them every day (like next to your desk, on your screensaver etc.)

Write your refined, bold dreams here:

....

....

....

....

....

....

....

....

....

....

PLANNING

18. No Excuses!

"All men dream, but not equally. Those who dream by night in the dusty recesses of their minds, wake in the day to find that it was vanity: but the **dreamers of the day** are dangerous men, for they may act on their dreams with open eyes, to make them possible. This I did."

- T. E Lawrence (Lawrence of Arabia)

Dreaming by itself is not enough. You have to put dreams into action. You must become a 'dreamer of the day', to quote Lawrence of Arabia, to make great things happen in your life. Getting in touch with your dream is the starting point, but you must move to creating a plan to make your dreams reality.

Another great movie I enjoyed is 'The First Grader' which tells a true story of Kimani Maruge, an 84-year-old Mau Mau Veteran (rebel/freedom fighters against the English rule in Kenya). Maruge is now an old man, his freedom fighter days 50 years behind him, but he's still poor and never has had an education. He receives an important letter, from the Office of The President of Kenya but he cannot read. When he hears an announcement on radio that there is to be free education for all in schools across the country, he sets out to enroll at the local primary school.

The 84-year-old is told that the school is for children and that he should just go home and 'rest in peace'. To which he responds with 'I'm not dead!' and promises to be a good pupil if given a chance. He is told that he can't enroll anyway because has no uniform. He sells a goat and a chicken to buy material to saw a uniform for himself. When he shows up in full uniform the teacher takes him in.

What ended up happening with Kimani Maruge in real life is that he became the oldest person to start primary school in history (Guinness World Record). He was invited to address the UN Millennium Development Summit in New York and boarded a plane for the first time and became an inspiration for educationists the world over.

Maruge was 84! Eighty-four years old but when an opportunity to make his lifelong dream of getting an education, he took it!

What's your excuse?

We all have excuses why we can't go after our dreams. I'm too old, I'm too young, I don't have the money, I don't have the energy and so on it goes. Your future begins to change the moment you give up your excuses. Think about your own excuses that are currently holding you back from going after the dreams you wrote down in the previous chapter. Are you willing to let your excuses determine your future? I hope your answer is no, so that we can get on to shattering your excuses right now.

When you visualize a great future, you have a DREAM, when you set targets to it you create a GOAL, but when you outline steps to get there, you have an ACTION PLAN

This is where goals come in. Goal-setting is about turning dreams into an action plan. As important as a dream may be, it is not enough, you must act to make it happen. You must be willing first to put together specific targets that you want to reach and then a plan to get you there. We do this all the time in our work, in our projects that we carry out, but when it comes to our own lives, we somehow don't think it's that important. Get rid of whatever excuses you might have and let's work on creating goals that move you to greatness.

Turn Your Dreams into Goals

Using the dreams, you laid out in the previous chapter, here is what you need to do to turn them into goals:

1. Take a piece of paper or a notebook and go to a quiet place, in your garden, park or behind a closed door.

2. Take the dreams you outlined in the previous chapter. Think about what you want, what will make you happy, what will make you a fulfilled person and the difference you want to make in the world around you.

3. For each dream category start writing your long-term goals (something specific you will do/achieve in 5-10 years). Example: *In the next 6 years I want to complete my PHD.*

4. For each dream category write your mid-term goal/s (3 years) and short term goals (six months).
   Example: *I will complete my MBA in the next 3 years (Mid-term). I will enroll at business school this summer (Short-term).*

5. Ask yourself what will your first steps be and commit to doing them. Like enrolling for that course, doing some research, getting a mentor, or opening an investment account and more. The key thing is to write down the steps to get you there, the more detail, the better

6. Allow these to sink in and refer to them often, once they are in your system you're on the right track. Your brain is an amazing thing; it's amazing what your subconscious will do when you have committed on paper to do something.

7. Put the deadlines on your calendar for each step. Unless it is committed and scheduled it might not happen. This is important especially for your short to medium goals.

> **"People with goals succeed because they know where they are going: it's simple as that."**
>
> **- Earl Nightingale**

Say goodbye to your excuses and start creating the future you've always wanted!

ACTION

19. Seize The Opportunities

"Those who succeed are those who walk through the door of opportunity when it swings open. But what is the secret to getting through the door of opportunity? Being outside the door when it swings open."

- Chris Widener

If you are still reading at this point, there are a few things we have discovered about you. You have dreams about where you want to go and who you want to be. You have specific goals that you have outlined and broken into long, mid and short terms and you have put some deadlines and scheduled them into your calendar. Am I right? Now what?

It's time for lights, camera, **ACTION**!

Maybe your dream is start your very own business and become your own boss. Wonderful! But I am sure that after settling on that specific goal and having the goals that go with that, the tricky part is getting going. I remember when I decided to start my own consulting firm at the age of 22. I was newly married, I had a steady job, but I was just in a JOB (Just Over Broke). We hardly had enough to live on after paying rent and transport. I knew that my idea and my passion for helping people could create a very fulfilling life and be financially rewarding.

But I was young, without money and no experience in business. So, I decided to equip myself for the person I wanted to be. I bought books on starting a business and attended courses and looked for a mentor. As I read and learned about the ins and outs of business, I started getting in touch with agencies that were available to help aspiring young entrepreneurs. The following year in the summer of 2003 while visiting Canada with my new young wife, I found the Open for Business CEED office in Halifax and got as much information from them as I could. They told me they had an office in Johannesburg, which I promptly connected with upon my return.

I got step-by-step support and guidance and even some funding to get my business registered. I was on my way and started trading that same year. Do you see the sequence?

Dream > Goal > Preparation > Action

Your dream must be crystal clear in your head - *I want to start my own business.* Then your goal – *I want to be incorporated within a year.* Then preparation – *equipping myself for making it happen.* Taking action – *registering my business and trading.*

Seizing the Opportunity of a Lifetime

Whether you unleash your greatness and become all that you can be, depends on whether you seize the opportunities when they come around. A lot of people who know where I came from, people who have seen my progress over the years often say to me "You are so lucky!" Many of them truly believe that I am where I am today because I have had a good fortune. But I see a totally different picture from my perspective.

Is it really luck? Well, Gary Player the famous South African golf legend told this story to Golf Digest in 2002:

I was practicing in a bunker down in Texas and this good old boy with a big hat stopped to watch. The first shot he saw me hit went in the hole. He said, "You got 50 bucks if you knock the next one in." I holed the next one. Then he says, "You got $100 if you hole the *next one." In it went for three in a row. As he peeled off the bills he said, "Boy, I've never seen anyone so lucky in my life." And I shot back, "Well, the harder I practice, the luckier I get."*

As I look back I do not believe that it was luck that brought me to where I am today, any more than I believe luck is responsible for your success. I have always lived my life by having a clear dream for where I want to go, planning to get there and taking action. When I was younger I didn't know this was what I was doing. I just did it.

When I heard a Salvation Army Brass Band as a young boy, I knew I wanted to play one of those instruments. So, when a young Salvation Army Officer became our pastor in our village, I signed up to learn playing a Tuba. It was old, broken and held together by wire and duct tape but, every week I made the 10km walk to learn to play that Tuba until I could play. When the opportunity came, I took it. Today, I can play Tuba, Trumpet and Guitar not by luck but by doing what it takes to learn and acquire that skill.

Writing Books and Traveling the World!

The school that I went to in Hlabisa did not have books, not enough anyway for all of us, we had to share 4 and sometimes 8 students to one book. This made it difficult to study for exams as we had to make plans to come together to learn outside of school if we wanted to pass. The first library I had at my school was when I was in grade 10. It was a cupboard of books that had been donated to the school.

I was thrilled when the new library was announced! It was to be housed within the teachers' staff room, which also doubled as a school hall for events. Most students simply didn't bother because of having to go to the teachers' staff room to access the library. Out of a school of over one thousand students only five of us took the time to get the books out. It changed my life!

I was still studying by candle light at night but now I was reading the Guinness Book of Records and being inspired about people who had done amazing things. I still had to fetch water from the river and look after cows but I was now dreaming about traveling to distant places and seeing the world. This little library opened a whole new world for me even as my circumstances remained the same. I was in the same place physically with my fellow students but I was living in a much larger world filled with possibility.

Today, I have authored 6 books and have travelled to so many places around the world, places I only dreamt of as a kid in Hlabisa. All because I seized the opportunity of lifetime in a lifetime of that opportunity. The little cupboard library became a window to the world that was far beyond my reality at that time. As I was being introduced to the wonders of The Chronicles of Narnia, the cupboard in the teachers' staffroom became my very own doorway to the Narnia of my own life.

> **"The opportunity of a lifetime must be seized within the lifetime of the opportunity." – Leonard Ravenhill**

So, no, they were wrong it's not luck that got me here but a clear dream, making a plan and seizing the opportunity when it came and taking action.

You can do the same, decide that you will prepare yourself for when the right opportunity comes along. Be ready with a dream in your heart, a goal in your head and an action plan in your diary. Do the work of turning your dreams into reality. Challenge yourself with higher goals than what you've been settling for and give up your excuses. You'll be surprised how close you are to your greatness.

What Opportunities Have You Overlooked?

What Will You Do To Grab The Opportunities You Have?

DARING

20. Create A Great Future

"The reasonable man adapts himself to the world: the unreasonable one persists in trying to adapt the world to himself. Therefore, all progress depends on the unreasonable man."

- George Bernard Shaw

How would our world look like without the great ones? The ones who dare to shape the world around them, and refuse to accept things as they are but rather push for what could be. Imagine if the early scientists decided to give up figuring out the physical and chemical world around us. If Thomas Edison simply said it's just too hard when he couldn't get the lightbulb idea to work or the electricity idea before that. If Henry Ford buckled under the pressure of the naysayers and didn't continue his pursuit of making a car for the common man.

Without the great ones, our world will be a smaller place indeed. Greatness is about pushing beyond the ordinary to create the extra-ordinary. Greatness is about asking questions and creating solutions. It is about shaping one's own life, but often driven by a passion to change many lives.

Never underestimate the power of the smallest person who has greatness inside of them. Because, no matter what they look like or what their background is, it's what's in them that makes all the difference. I believe you have greatness inside of you. I believe that you are meant for so much more than what many settle for. You have ideas that can make you successful but more importantly ideas that can change the world in one way or another.

Dare to Be Unreasonable

Our whole lives we are told to follow the beaten path and do what everybody else does. But, you are not everybody else, you are you. Endowed with incredible gifts and abilities that if you dared to explore them closely, you would be astounded at what you have. If you dared to do the unreasonable thing and create what you have been dreaming about, you'll taste and experience greatness.

Challenge yourself now to start a new chapter in your life. This chapter is going be called GREATNESS. Not by anybody else's standards but your own. Decide that you will be more daring, more unreasonable, and more hopeful about your future.

You now have the right keys on your side.

1. Be Who You Be

You have explored the person you are and the person you want to be. I hope that the work you did in the first chapters has helped you to get in touch with yourself. You are unique and have a special contribution to the world. You have amazing gifts and talents that you can develop and master.

You have identified the things that make you stand out and have a better understanding of your purpose or your *WHY*. Understanding this first key to unleashing your greatness means that you will find more confidence in yourself and Be Who You Be Maaan!

2. Live Your Values

You took the time to explore, 'What's On Your T-shirt', unearthing your own values that shape the quality of life you want to lead. By defining your own values, you set a foundation that will ensure that your life can withstand whatever storms and challenges you will undoubtedly face as you continue to pursue your best life. Your behaviors based on those values will determine the character and the direction your life takes.

As you continue with life I hope that you will continually refer to your own Green Apron Book in shaping your reputation.

3. Pursue Excellence

Remember, Good Enough Is Not Good Enough! So stop settling for less than what is possible for you. How high you go, will be determined by how much effort you're willing to put in compared to your peers. Like Michael Jordan, it's not only your talent that will determine your success but whether you are willing to go on the extra mile.

Always take full ownership of your work, your life and contribution. Never be a candidate for "It's Not My Job Award'. Take pride in what you put your mind and your hands on as if your own reputation depended on it, because it does. Build a cathedral, a dream and not merely doing a job or earning a living. Build a legacy with every task you undertake.

4. Unleash A Winning Attitude

Only you can decide how you show up. Your attitude towards the world and your work will determine the results you get. Choose a winning attitude and do not be driven by feelings or your conditions, but by your beliefs.

Let your attitude help you choose your response to whatever you face going forward. Choose to be a thermostat and not merely a thermometer. Be in control of your own response to what happens to you, don't just reflect what the world throws at you. Believe in yourself always, because you have what it takes!

5. Create Your Future

Never lose sight of your dreams again. Your dreams are your own windows to a future that is possible for you. No one else but you, can rob you of that future, so stay committed to owning your own dreams. Be clear about what you want in your life, articulate it and review it regularly.

Decide that there will be no more excuses for you as you have put your dreams into goals and action plans. You have the power to make your dreams reality, just plan and take action.

Open your eyes to the opportunities that will be presented throughout your journey. Become an opportunity seeker and always be ready by the door of opportunity.

> **"The best way to predict the future is to invent it!"**
>
> **– Allan Kay**

Dare to believe in your greatness and a great future. Because you can, because you must and the world needs you now to Unleash Your Greatness and Be Who You Be Maaaan!

No Turning Back!

The worst thing you can do after reading this book is to go back to business as usual. No, not for you! You must decide for yourself that you will, starting now, do your best to live out these five keys to being extraordinary. Decide to close the chapter of your comfort zone for the possibility of a great future in all spheres of your life.

The story is told about **Hernán Cortés** who was the commander of the Spanish mission to conquer the Aztec Empire. He set sail with his crew, battling many challenges at sea, including storms and pirates, finally he landed in modern day Vera Cruz. Many of his troops were tired and sick and many wanted to just go back home. But **Cortés** gave a stunning order *"Burn the Boats!"*

No longer could his men entertain the idea of going back to what they were used to or their comfort zones. The only way now was forward, and on to victory!

I am not a fan of imperial colonialism, not by a long shot, but I appreciate the bold move that was taken in order to secure victory. In your own journey to your greatness you are going to have to burn some boats. No more dreaming of an ordinary life but make yours extraordinary. You will face many challenges that will make you want to quit, but if you persevere, great things will happen.

Thank you, for investing your time and energy in going through this book and making it a companion on your journey to greatness. My hope is that this will be more that an inspiration but an activation to a truly remarkable way of being and seeing your world.

May you rise to all you were meant to be, because all of us can be great!

The Adinkra Symbol for Greatness.

Adinkra are visual symbols, originally created by the *Ashanti*, that represent concepts or aphorisms. *Adinkra* are used extensively in African fabrics and pottery. They are incorporated into walls and other architectural features.

ABOUT THE AUTHOR

Buhle Dlamini is a global inspirational business speaker. He speaks at corporate conferences worldwide on unleashing greatness, leadership, organizational culture and managing diversity with his unforgettable humor, stories, and impeccable business acumen.

Raised in a rural village in South Africa, he beat the odds to become a top South African entrepreneur and global speaker. He met and worked with iconic leaders like Nelson Mandela and received an award from Desmond Tutu. He weaves his personal story of success over adversity in all his presentations connecting with audiences at a personal and professional level. He is based in Canada, with an office in South Africa, he regularly travels between the two countries, the USA, and many other destinations around the world.

Apart from running his own businesses, he is passionately involved in social causes with organizations like The Salvation Army, in which he's a lifelong active member. He also co-founded Columba Leadership in South Africa that is helping young leaders from schools in tough communities to reach their potential. He is the founding member of Heartlines a mass media values initiative that uses movies and stories to communicate and promote good values.

He is married to Stacey and they have four children, Bijou, Nhlanhla, Trinity and Khaya.

www.buhledlamini.com

Buhle Dlamini

Made in United States
Orlando, FL
22 July 2024

49421355R00065